SM

This Book Was Provided Through
ESEA Title VI, Fiscal Year '02
Acct. #24142-04-09-001-53170

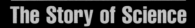

The Story of Science

# Eyes on the Universe

## by George Reed

BENCHMARK BOOKS

MARSHALL CAVENDISH
NEW YORK

Series Editor: Roy A. Gallant

Series Consultants:

LIFE SCIENCES
Dr. Edward J. Kormondy
Chancellor and Professor of Biology (retired)
University of Hawaii—Hilo/West Oahu

PHYSICAL SCIENCES
Dr. Jerry LaSala
Department of Physics
University of Southern Maine

Benchmark Books
Marshall Cavendish Corporation
99 White Plains Road
Tarrytown, NY 10591-9001

Library of Congress Cataloging-in-Publication Date

Reed, George, 1939-
        Eyes on the universe / by George Reed.
               p. cm. – (The story of science)
        Includes bibliographical references and index.
        ISBN 0-7614-1154-2
1. Astronomy—Juvenile literature. [1. Astronomy.] I. Title. II. Series.

QB46.R397 2000
520—dc21                                      00-031527

Photo research by Linda Sykes Picture Research, Hilton Head, SC
Diagrams on pp. 8, 16, 17, 19, 21, 24, 26, 33, 34, 51, 52, 53, 55, 56, 59, 62, by Jeannine L. Dickey
Cover illustration: NASA/JPL/California Institute of Technology.
Title Page: a and b: (nebulas): Material created with support to AURA/StScI from NASA contract NAS5-26555; c: (Hubble drawing): NASA.
Photo credits: Peter Lloyd/National Geographic Image Collection: 7; www.arttoday.com: 11; © Ted Spiegel/CORBIS: 14; Corbis-Bettman: 18, 44, 57; The Grainger Collection: 20, 23; Uffizi Gallery, Florence/the art archive: 25; The Royal Society/the art archive: 30; British Library/the art archive: 31; Jean-Leon Huens/National Geographic Image Collection: 36, 41; AKG, London: 39; Material created with support to AURA/StScI from NASA contract NAS5-26555: 46; AIP Emilio Segre Visual Archives, Shapley Collection: 58; Jonathan Blair/National Geographic Image Collection: 63; Infrared Processing and Analysis Center Caltech/JPL: 64 (right); Bill Schoening, Vanessa Harvey/ REU program/AURA/NOAO/NSF, all rights reserved: 64 (left); NASA: 66, 67, 68; Courtesy of the NAIX-Aricibo Observatory, a facility of the NSF—David Parker/Science Photo Library: 73.

Printed in Hong Kong
6 5 4 3 2 1

For Kelly Reed Cavanaugh
Kyle Reed Cowper


*Oh, the Places You'll Go!*
—Dr. Seuss

# Contents

# One

# Why Did Astronomy Begin?

People have always been curious about their world, but just how curious often depended on their needs. Did the earliest stargazers look with curiosity at the sky and try to understand the Universe beyond their horizon? Probably not. To survive, they had more practical and important things to attend to. Simply to satisfy their curiosity would require leisure time, and leisure time was probably in short supply. Even so, they had to notice certain changes that took place in the sky as they went about their lives as hunters of animals and gatherers of berries and seeds.

*An Egyptian myth tells of a sacred boat that carried the Sun god Ra across the heavenly ocean every day. Each morning it rose in the east and in evening set below the western horizon.*

## The Measure of Time

Astronomy probably began as a search for a way to measure time. Time was important for successful planting, harvesting, and hunting activities. Time is the counting of successive intervals between an event that occurs repeatedly—between one sunrise and the next, between one full moon and the next, and so on. Our sense of time demands that these intervals be equal. Only the sky could provide such recurring events to measure time. So astronomy started with the need to measure time, and astronomy's most important gift to civilization became time.

The measure of time began in the eastern sky with the rising of the Sun. This was the beginning event of successive day counts. The problem with day counts is that they come too rapidly. The numbers grow too fast. A longer period between events that happen again and again is needed to measure time over many days.

The changing phases of the Moon provided a longer natural cycle as a time count. The time from new moon to the next new

moon, or from full moon to the next full moon, provided the beginning of successive "moonth" counts. This is how we measure a month. It was easy to learn that it took 29 ½ days for every cycle of the moon count. But the old sky watchers sometimes needed still longer time cycles. They knew there was also a seasonal cycle, but the seasonal cycle was not easy to measure.

A shadow-casting stick rising straight up from the ground was used to keep track of the seasons. It was called a *gnomon*. The gnomon was a crude sundial, and it was the first astronomical instrument invented. The direction of the shadow cast by the Sun

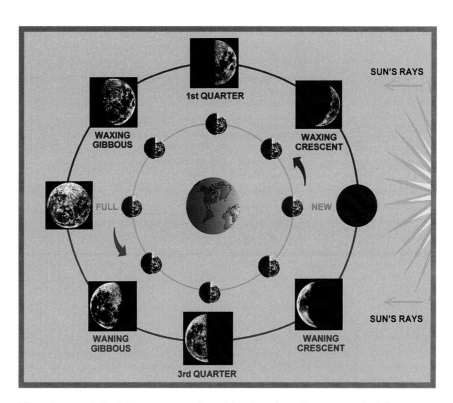

*The phases of the Moon are produced by the changing amount of the lighted surface of the Moon that we can see from Earth. Notice that one half of the Moon is always lighted and one half is always dark. Also notice that the same side of the Moon always faces Earth.*

changed at sunrise and sunset during the seasons. So did the length of the shadow cast by the Sun at noon, when the Sun was highest in the sky.

The movement of the gnomon shadow during daytime was used to divide the day into hours. The gnomon's yearly cycle of shadows measured between 365 and 366 day-counts. It was close to the cycle of seasons. This was the beginning of successive solar year counts.

## The First Calendars—The First Astronomers

A calendar is a method of organizing time. Day counts, moon cycle counts, and solar year counts can be used. Unfortunately, the calendars that used day counts, moon counts, and season counts did not work well together. Twenty-nine and one-half days equaled one "moonth," and 12.4 "moonths" equaled one 365-day seasonal year. That meant that the lunar year was 11 days shorter than the seasonal year.

Those appointed to be keepers of the early calendars had to observe the rising and setting of the Sun, the phases of the Moon, and other celestial, or sky, events. As they did, they would have observed the sky in detail and become aware of slowly changing and unpredictable celestial events. For instance, *constellations* of different names and outlines were created by early sky watchers all over the world from patterns formed by bright stars. Some of these constellations come into view only during certain seasons. The earliest known list of constellations contained 44. It was provided by the Greek poet Aratus of Soli, who lived around 270 B.C. Since that time constellations have been added and subtracted from the list. Today the official number is 88.

The early sky watchers looked on all objects in the sky as stars, except for the Sun and Moon. The constellations were made up of the *fixed stars*. Their stars were "fixed" because they could not be seen to move in relation to one another. The five starlike objects we know today as planets were called *wandering stars* because they were seen to move among the background of fixed stars. Because of their long tails, comets were called *hairy stars*, and meteors were called *shooting stars*. Astronomical knowledge grew and was passed from sky watcher to sky watcher by word of mouth from one generation to the next. Information was not written until some 5,000 years ago.

## Ancient Astronomy and Archaeology

We do not have a written history of the very beginnings of astronomy. However, we do have evidence that ancient peoples of Africa, Central America, and other places around the globe used their knowledge of sky events for practical purposes. The study of such early uses of astronomy is called *archaeoastronomy*. Archaeoastronomy has uncovered many examples of cultures that used star positions to align buildings and monuments.

In Egypt the pyramids and tombs of dead pharaohs were built on the western bank of the Nile River, the side where the Sun died at the end of the day. Temples for the living were built on the eastern side of the river, the side of the Sun's rebirth each morning. The Great Pyramid of Khufu at Giza was built around 2700 B.C. The more than two million limestone blocks, each weighing more than two tons, are accurately aligned within a few degrees of the north, east, south, and west points on the horizon.

The Egyptian pharaoh Ramses II, who lived around 1250 B.C., built a temple at Abu Simbel that was aligned to a special sunrise direction along the eastern horizon to celebrate two special days. The two days were February 22, his birthday, and October 22, the day honoring the beginning of his rule. Light from the rising

Sun on these days flooded a corridor 200 feet (61 meters) long and illuminated a statue of Ramses II seated between two gods.

One of the most famous astronomical sites in the world is England's Stonehenge, built around 2000 B.C. by a people who had not yet even invented the wheel. We call them the Beaker People because they left many beakers in their trash pits.

*Stonehenge is a curious structure of enormous stones arranged in a double circle. Built around 1800 B.C., it is thought to have been used as a combination religious center and astronomical observatory. Inset shows how the original arrangement of stones might have been.*

They managed to use logs as rollers to move 50-ton, 15-foot-long (5-meter) stones over hilly distances of 25 miles (40 kilometers) to build Stonehenge. Smaller stones weighing 5 tons were brought on rafts along the English coast from distances as far away as 250 miles (400 kilometers). In 1966 astronomer Gerald Hawkins discovered that Stonehenge was probably an elaborate solar and lunar calendar.

The measure of time wasn't the only use of the sky for practical purposes. All early peoples looked for *omens*, or signs, that supposedly allowed them to tell the future. The use of the sky for this purpose is called *astrology*. Astrology began in ancient Babylonia some 4,000 or more years ago. The sky watchers of ancient Babylonia viewed the heavens from great pyramid temples that offered them a view from high above the fertile plains of what is now Iraq. The Babylonians used astrology to try to predict future events that affected the state and its rulers. The Greeks later tried to use the sky positions of the Sun, Moon, and planets at birth to predict a person's personality. Many people confuse astronomy and astrology because they both deal with the sky. Astronomers were also astrologers until almost 300 years ago. As we will see, *astronomy* eventually became a science asking questions about the Universe. Astrology did not.

Eventually sky watchers began to ask new questions about the details of the Universe. How far away are the stars? What makes them shine? It was then that the sky watchers became astronomers.

# Two

# The Greeks Build a Universe

In addition to being curious about the world, people want their world to be orderly and understandable. This is especially true of astronomers. Any new knowledge that came along in ancient times had to somehow fit into their comfortable view of the world. This meant fitting new facts and new observations into their view of a world that was influenced by a mixture of myths, magic, and superstition. For centuries the planets and Sun had been looked on as gods, and the heavens were where the gods lived.

The most important group of new thinkers to come along were the ancient Greeks. They began to ask questions about *how* the Universe was organized. These astronomers searched for answers that did not depend on old stories and superstitious beliefs.

## The First Models of the Universe

It was the early Greeks around 370 B.C. who first began to build mental models of the Universe that were closer to what we know as science today. The Greeks were philosophers. They were also good at mathematics and geometry. They wanted to know what made the sky change. Their idea of the Universe started as a group of educated guesses to explain what they saw in the night sky from year to year. The Greek model of the Universe was based on explanations backed by a new way of thinking.

The famous philosopher Plato (c. 428–347 B.C.) began the search for an accurate model of the Universe around 400 B.C. He did not like astronomy, but he loved geometry. At the Academy he established in 387 B.C., Plato gave his students a homework assignment that was no easy task. He asked them to *save the phenomena.* He wanted them to think of a model of a Universe that would explain everything they saw in the night sky. There were certain things that Plato insisted the model must include. The first was the "commonsense" idea that Earth did not move. It stood still at the very center of a great sphere of unknown material. All the stars were somehow attached to the outer part of this celestial sphere. The movement of the sphere moved the stars, just as we see them move across the sky on any clear night. Plato's second "commonsense" idea was that the Sun, Moon, and planets

*Plato the teacher (left) talking to his student Aristotle, as shown in a wall painting, the* School of Athens, *by the Italian painter Raphael. Classes were held as the students followed the walking Plato to discuss ideas about science and philosophy. Aristotle lived around 350 B.C.*

circled Earth. Anyone could see this just by watching the sky.

Plato pictured the Universe as a set of nested spheres. The Sun was attached to one sphere, the Moon to another, and each planet had its own sphere. As the largest celestial sphere turned, it somehow also spun the smaller spheres of the Sun, Moon, and planets around Earth. All motion was even, and all motion followed perfect circles. Plato thought circles and spheres were the most perfect of all geometric shapes. This was not surprising. A sign above his Academy "office" door read, "Let no one enter here who knows of no geometry." It was a warning to his students. Plato's ideal, unchanging Universe with Earth at the center influenced other models of the Universe.

## An Onion Universe

Aristotle (384–322 B.C.) was Plato's most famous student and became the most famous philosopher of ancient Greece. He wrote books on many subjects, from astronomy to zoology. In fact, his ideas are still studied today. Aristotle tried to solve Plato's assignment to save the phenomena by trying to improve the accuracy of Plato's model. He used 56 moving crystal spheres, one inside the other. Aristotle's model has been described as an "onion universe" because his spheres touched.

He added ideas to his model that had nothing to do with astronomy. He divided the Universe into two parts separated by the orbit of the Moon. This side of the Moon you find change, such as growth and decay, birth and death. Beyond the Moon and out to the sphere of the fixed stars, you do not find change. Everything there is perfect and eternal, so there can be no change. Aristotle also believed the entire rest of the Universe was contained in the outermost sphere, the celestial sphere. Nothing existed beyond the last sphere of the fixed stars.

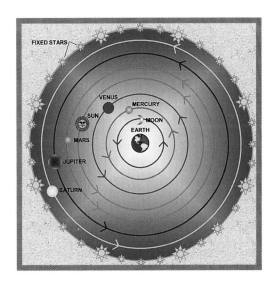

Aristotle's model of the Universe is a geocentric model of spheres, meaning that Earth stood still at the center. The Sun, Moon, and planets all circled Earth as their spinning spheres carried them around Earth. The stars were fixed to the outermost sphere. According to Aristotle, nothing existed outside the last sphere.

Aristotle's model of the Universe became the accepted one for almost 2,000 years. How was one man able to have such a strong influence that lasted so long? For one thing, Aristotle's ideas strongly appealed to common sense. You could see the same sky moving overhead year after year. For more than 2,000 years students were taught to study and quote Aristotle. He was the final authority on all things. If Aristotle said that Earth stands still and is the center of the Universe, then it must be so. His model came to be called a *geocentric* (meaning "Earth-centered") model of the Universe.

Does this mean that *everyone* agreed with Aristotle? No. Aristarchus, from the island of Samos near the coast of Asia Minor, disagreed. Around 325 B.C. he said that all the motions of the Sun, Moon, stars, and planets could be explained just as well by an Earth that: 1) *rotated*, or spun around; and 2) *revolved*, or circled, around the Sun. Although he was right, he was right at the wrong time in history. Any idea that could not be tested, and that did not agree with the great Aristotle, was doomed. A model that had Earth revolving around the Sun predicted that the stars should show a shift in position called *parallax*. But no such shift could be seen. Aristarchus had few followers.

**P**arallax is easy to understand if you do this: Shut one *eye*, hold up your thumb a few inches from your open *eye* and sight along your thumb to a distant object. Hold your thumb still and wink your eyes back and forth. The jumping back and forth of your thumb is a parallax shift.

# Parallax:
## Now You See It, Now You Don't

Now repeat what you just did but this time with your thumb held out at arm's length. The farther your thumb, the smaller the parallax shift. If Earth revolved around the Sun, then a parallax shift should be seen among the stars. Unfortunately for Aristarchus, no such shift could be observed. Aristarchus correctly said that the stars were too far away for a parallax shift to be observed.

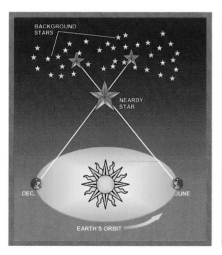

*The parallax shift of a nearby star was proof that Earth and the other planets revolved around the Sun. A nearby star's position against the background stars is photographed in December. Six months later, when Earth is halfway around its orbit, the same star's position against the background stars is photographed again. When the two photographs are compared, the nearby star seems to have shifted position to the left. If Earth did not circle the Sun, there would be no parallax shift of the nearby star.*

# Aristotle's Model Becomes Too Difficult

Aristotle's model of the Universe did not die with him in 322 B.C. Others tried to improve its accuracy without destroying Aristotle's basic beliefs. The goal was always to create a model that would explain all that was seen in the night sky.

Around 150 B.C., the last of the great astronomers of ancient Greece, Hipparchus, was watching the sky from his observatory on the Greek island of Rhodes in the Aegean Sea. The observatory had only simple instruments to measure angles. Hipparchus first became interested in the night sky in 134 B.C. when a *nova*, meaning a "new" star, appeared in the night sky. What he saw was really the light from an exploding star. However, no one knew this at the time. Hipparchus's interest in the stars led him to become the most skilled sky watcher of ancient Greece. He made the first sky map and celestial globe showing the positions of 850 stars. He was also the first astronomer to rank stars by their *apparent brightness*, or how bright they appear to the eye when compared with each other. He called the brightest stars first-magnitude stars and the faintest stars he could see sixth-magnitude stars. Hipparchus also invented a new way to map his star positions. It was very much like the lines of latitude and longitude that we use on maps today to locate positions of cities and countries. His star-brightness

*Hipparchus, who lived around 150 B.C. was among the first observational astronomers who kept records of the night sky for future astronomers. He measured the positions and brightness of 850 stars and produced the first large catalog of stars. Here the height of a star is measured by using an instrument called a cross-staff.*

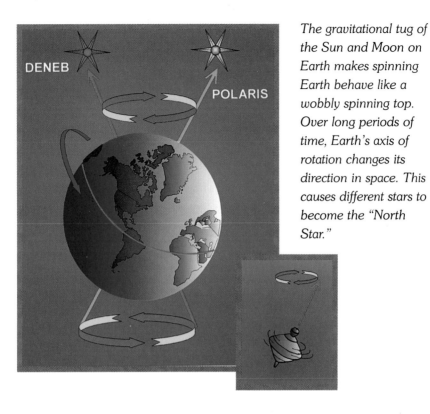

DENEB

POLARIS

*The gravitational tug of the Sun and Moon on Earth makes spinning Earth behave like a wobbly spinning top. Over long periods of time, Earth's axis of rotation changes its direction in space. This causes different stars to become the "North Star."*

system and sky-coordinate system are still in use today.

Hipparchus's work led to a surprising discovery. He noticed that some of his star positions did not agree with star positions reported 50 years earlier. He thought it was because the north pole of the sky probably had moved. The stars were rotating around a different point in the sky. Actually it was Earth that had moved, but that would not be explained until the time of Isaac Newton—almost 1,850 years later. This wobbly motion of Earth is caused by the gravity pull of the Sun and Moon. It is called *precession*.

## The Great Ptolemy

Claudius Ptolemaeus (c. A.D. 100–c. 170) was born in the city of Ptolemais on the Nile River in Egypt. His workplace was the great library and museum in Alexandria, and he observed from the city of Canopus, a city named for a bright star in the constellation Carina. Around A.D. 150, Ptolemy, as he is better known, wrote the most important astronomy book up to his time. He improved on Aristotle's geocentric model, but only by making it even more complex. For instance, each planet was placed on a small circle, called an *epicycle*, that moved with a constant motion around a point on a larger circle, called the *deferent*. The larger circle moved with constant motion around an unmoving Earth. This complex Ferris wheel model helped explain the puzzling "backward," or *retrograde*, motion of the planets from time to time. Ptolemy added a total of 40 epicycles to Aristotle's geocentric model of the Universe. It became extremely complex and difficult to use.

From Ptolemy's death around A.D. 170 until the 1500s, almost nothing new was added to our knowledge of the sky. Most astronomy and astrology books were lost or destroyed. After Ptolemy, religion, not science, became the major concern of scholars. Astronomy was used only when it could support religious ideas.

The very influential Catholic priest, Thomas Aquinas (1225–1274), added Aristotle's and Ptolemy's astronomy and other ideas to Christian beliefs. His important and well-studied book was called *Summa theologica*. The title means the

*CLAVDE PTOLOMEE PELVSIEN.*
*Chap. 41.*

*Much of what is known today about ancient astronomers comes from Ptolemy's great book,* Almagest, *published around A.D. 150. The book would remain the most influential astronomy text for 1,300 years.*

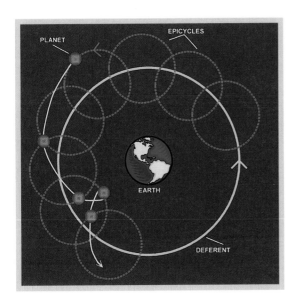

*Ptolemy used epicycles and deferents to explain the observed looping motions of planets as they moved across the night sky. Earth was located at the center of the circle of moving deferents. As an epicycle circle moved along its deferent circle, it carried a planet along in a path that appeared to trace a loop to an observer on Earth.*

"Summation of Theology." The publication of this book was a very important event because from that time on, any attack on the idea of Earth standing motionless at the center of the Universe was an attack on religious beliefs.

How did educated people feel about the geocentric model of Aristotle and Ptolemy? King Alfonso X (1221–1284) of Spain was called "the Wise." He hired 50 astronomers to work for 10 years to produce a list of future planet positions for astrologers to use. The more the astronomers worked, the more upset King Alfonso became. He thought the model of the Universe of Aristotle and Ptolemy was too complex. Alfonso "the Wise" then unwisely declared, "If God had consulted me before He made the Universe, I could have given him some very good advice." His son used these words that criticized God to force his father to give up his throne.

A Polish astronomer named Nicolaus Copernicus had the same idea about the Universe, but he did something about it.

# Three

# A Revolution and a Telescope

Revolutions sometimes begin in strange places and in strange ways. One—the Copernican Revolution—began with the publication of a book in 1543. Its title was *On the Revolutions of the Heavenly Spheres*, and it was the first important astronomy book to appear in 1,300 years. But more important, it challenged Ptolemy by showing a new way to predict the future positions of the planets. The book was written by Nicolaus Copernicus (1473–1543), a timid official from the Frombork Cathedral in what is now Poland. After a delay of 36 years, friends eventually persuaded Copernicus to publish his book. He saw the first printed copy as he lay dying.

## Copernicus Makes a Choice

Copernicus observed the night sky from a tower in the defense wall surrounding the Frombork Cathedral. He used only instruments he built himself by following descriptions given by Ptolemy 1,300 years earlier.

*Nicolaus Copernicus, who died in 1543, observed the sky and wrote his book* On the Revolutions of the Heavenly Spheres *from a cathedral tower in Frombork, Poland. Only 100 people are thought to have read his book in the first 50 years after it was published. Even so, the book greatly influenced astronomers. Not even Copernicus read the completed book because he died on the day it was printed. The book started astronomy's greatest revolution— belief that Earth and all the other planets revolve around the Sun.*

Copernicus was not a revolutionary in his thinking. He was not even an original thinker. He made a choice, not a discovery, when he decided to "Save the Phenomena" by trying to show that Aristarchus had been right all along—that Earth and the other planets all circled the Sun. His model of the Universe was called *heliocentric*, meaning "Sun-centered." Further, Copernicus said that Earth spun around on its axis like a top. It was that spinning motion, he explained, that made the Sun and stars only seem to parade across the sky from east to west.

Copernicus had to face many of the same criticisms that Aristarchus had faced. Why didn't the stars show a parallax shift? Copernicus answered that the stars were too far away. If Earth

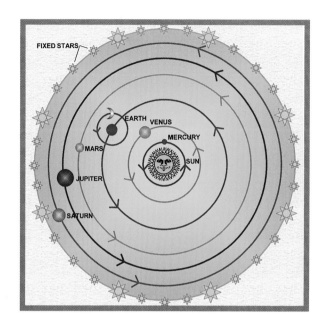

*Copernicus's model of the Universe was a heliocentric model of spheres. The Sun was stationary in the center. Earth and all the other planets circled the Sun as their spheres spun around the central Sun. The Moon circled Earth. The outer sphere of "fixed" stars did not move.*

rotated, then why didn't a strong wind blow constantly from the east? Copernicus answered that Earth and air move together. If Earth revolved around the Sun, then why was the Moon not left behind? Copernicus answered that the Moon moved in a steady circular motion around Earth and was carried along with Earth. None of the answers were very satisfactory to his critics.

Which model—the Earth-centered or Sun-centered—of the Universe could be shown to be the correct one? At the time of Copernicus, neither. This was to the advantage of Aristotle and Ptolemy. Copernicus's heliocentric model would begin a revolution with very little ammunition. Copernicus knew this. And this was probably why he waited so long to release his book to the world.

As it turned out, the Copernican heliocentric model was neither more accurate nor simpler than the old geocentric model of Ptolemy. However the Copernican model did predict that Venus would go through both crescent and gibbous phases, Ptolemy's model predicted only crescent phases. A *crescent* phase shows less than half of a disk lighted by the Sun. A *gibbous* phase shows more than half of a disk lighted by the Sun. But since it was impossible to see Venus change phases without the aid of a telescope, that was hardly an important point at the time.

## The Telescope Looks at New Worlds

The invention of the telescope produced the most important revolution in the history of astronomy. It was supposedly invented in 1608 in the shop of the Dutch eyeglasses-maker Hans Lippershey, who died in 1619. The story tells about a young assistant who accidentally looked through two lenses with one eye and saw faraway objects appear closer. Lippershey is given credit for the invention because he was the first to suggest that it could be used as a military device for seeing faraway ships. But it was Galileo Galilei (1564–1642), an Italian professor-inventor-astronomer who turned Lippershey's "spy glass" into a wondrous tool of astronomy. As a new eye on the Universe, it would reveal wonders that many found hard to believe. Some even said that Galileo had "bewitched" his telescope to show things that were not real.

Galileo was strongly on the side of Copernicus.

*In the early 1600s Galileo supported Copernicus's idea of a Universe with the Sun at the center. He was the first to use a telescope to observe the Moon, planets, and stars and report the marvels his telescope revealed. Many did not believe him at first. The Catholic church placed him under house arrest for the rest of his life and forbade him to teach that Earth revolved around the Sun. It took the church some 400 years to finally admit that it had been wrong to punish Galileo.*

He was also a champion of the idea that knowledge should be obtained by asking questions of nature and performing experiments. He did not believe that ideas about the Universe should be based on Bible Scriptures, the teachings of the Church, or the authority of Aristotle. Galileo was the first of what we would today call a scientist. He is often called the "father of experimental science" because of the importance he placed on experiments.

In 1609 Galileo turned his newly made telescope toward the heavens and changed our view of the world forever. He studied the hazy band of light called the *Milky Way*. The ancient Greeks had been mystified by it and in their myths said it was milk spilled by the goddess Juno as she nursed the infant Hercules. Galileo at once saw that the milky band across the sky was made up of countless stars. Did this mean that the Universe was larger than anyone had ever thought and that the stars were actually too far away for a parallax shift to be easily observed? Galileo said yes.

He next pointed his telescope at Jupiter, and what he saw amazed him. Jupiter had four orbiting worlds, or moons. These natural satellites were not left behind as Jupiter moved

*Observations of Jupiter 1610*

| | |
|---|---|
| | ◐ ✳ ✳ |
| 30 | ✳ ✳ ◐　✳ |
| 2 | ◐ ✳ ✳　✳ |
| 3 | ◐ ✳　✳ |
| 3 | ✳ ◐　✳ |
| 4 | ✳ ◐ ✳ ✳ |
| 6 | ✳ ✳ ◐　✳ |
| 8 | ✳ ✳ ✳　◐ |
| 10 | ✳　✳　✳ ◐　✳ |
| 11 | ✳　✳　◐　✳ |
| 12 | ✳　◐ ✳ |
| 13 | ✳　✳ ✳◐ |
| 14 | ✳ ✳ ✳　◐ ✳ |
| 15 | ✳ ✳ ◐ |
| 16 | ✳ ◐ ✳ ✳ ✳ |
| 17 | ✳ ◐ ✳　✳ |
| 18 | ✳◐ ✳ ✳ ✳ |
| 21 | ✳ ✳　◐ ✳ ✳ |
| 24 | ✳ ✳　◐　✳ |
| 25 | ✳ ✳ ◐　　✳ |
| 29 | ✳ ✳　◐ |
| 30 | ✳ ✳ ◐　✳ |

*Galileo discovered four natural satellites, or moons, in orbit around Jupiter. The numbers at left are days of the month. On the 30th, for example, Galileo saw two moons to the left of Jupiter and one to the right. On the 16th, he saw one moon to the left and three to the right. The moons always moved right along with Jupiter. Galileo said that this showed Earth's Moon could also move right along with Earth as Earth traveled around the Sun.*

against the background stars. Did this mean that Earth's Moon orbited the planet without being left behind as Earth revolved around the Sun? Galileo said yes.

Galileo also studied images of the Sun with his telescope, something he later regretted because it may have led to his blindness. He saw dark spots that appeared and disappeared on the Sun. He followed the motion of larger, longer-lasting sunspots and discovered the Sun rotated once in a little less than a month. Did this mean that Aristotle's teaching that the Sun was perfect, unblemished, and unchanging was wrong? Galileo said yes.

He also pointed his telescope at the Moon and discovered that it was not perfectly smooth, as Aristotle had taught. It had Earthlike features such as mountains, valleys, craters, and what looked like seas. Did this mean that Aristotle's teaching that the Moon was perfectly smooth and round was wrong? Galileo said yes. Aristotle was wrong again.

Finally, Galileo carefully studied Venus to find out if Copernicus was right about its phases. He saw Venus in the crescent phase and in gibbous phases. This meant that Venus had to orbit the Sun, as Copernicus predicted. It did not orbit Earth, as Aristotle and Ptolemy had taught. In Galileo's eyes, the Copernican model was a more accurate way than the Aristotelian-Ptolemaic model to "Save the Phenomena."

## Galileo Says YES! The Church Says NO!

Did everyone now accept Copernicus's Sun-centered model? No. Old ideas tend to die slowly. There were questions of the "truth" of what Galileo claimed to see through this device of the Devil that was called a telescope. In fact, some disbelievers even refused to look through Galileo's telescope. They wondered why Aristotle, who was supposed to know all things, did not invent the telescope if the telescope was so important. And who was this Galileo to challenge the Bible and the teachings of the Church?

Galileo could not prove that Earth rotated on its axis or revolved around the Sun. He was acting on "blind faith" in trying to overturn the long-accepted geocentric model of the Universe. This was one reason for his difficulties with the Roman Catholic Church. Another reason was that Galileo was a very outspoken man who made many enemies. Galileo's problem with the Roman Catholic Church had little to do with whether Earth or the Sun was the center of the Universe. It was a battle over authority, not science versus religion. On whose authority was the design of the Universe to be determined? Was it to be determined by Galileo's telescope observations, or the Church's and Aristotle's teaching? Galileo thought the Church should tell people "how to go to heaven, not how the heavens go." In the end Galileo lost the battle. He was forced to say he had changed his views, and that he did not believe in the Sun-centered Universe. But he did.

The battle eventually was decided in favor of the Sun-centered model of the Universe. But it took some of the most unusual astronomers to win the long, slow war. An astronomer without a nose, a dwarf jester, an astronomer with extremely bad eyesight, and a young student under an apple tree are only part of the story.

# Four

# New Tools for Astronomers

The work of Copernicus and Galileo had convinced many astronomers of the early 1600s of the truthfulness of the Earth's spinning on its axis and circling the Sun. But proof would be a long time coming. Meanwhile three very unlikely individuals enter our story—Tycho Brahe, Johannes Kepler, and Isaac Newton. They were to provide the tools to break the Copernican model free of Ptolemy's cumbersome and inaccurate epicycles.

## Tycho's Castle of the Heavens

Tycho Brahe (1546–1601) was a Danish astronomer who died before the telescope was invented. Born and raised a nobleman, Tycho lived in two worlds. He enjoyed the comfort and wealth that came with his noble birth, but he wanted his life to have a worthwhile purpose. His father wanted him to study law. This was a "proper" profession for a young nobleman, but Tycho had a different idea. He put aside his law books and turned his attention to mathematics and the stars. Unfortunately, he was a better

*The Danish astronomer Tycho Brahe, about 1575, became the keenest observer of the heavens since the time of Hipparchus. It is hard to look at a portrait of Tycho without noticing his nose. He wore a false nose because of a duel fought over a math problem during his student days. The nose was made of a mixture of gold, silver, and copper and was painted a flesh color.*

mathematician than swordsman. Tycho lost his nose during a duel in a foggy graveyard because another student challenged his mathematical abilities. Forever after, he wore a false nose made of a mixture of gold, silver, and copper that was painted a flesh color.

Tycho was the greatest naked-eye astronomer of all astronomers up to his time. One night in 1572 he noticed a new star in the constellation Cassiopeia the Queen. It was a nova, an exploding star like the one that first interested Hipparchus more than 1,400 years earlier. Tycho carefully studied the changes in the brightness and position of the new star until it disappeared a year later. His published report, *On the New Star*, fixed his reputation in the world of astronomy and brought him to the attention of King Frederick II of Denmark. The proud king gave Tycho the island of Hven near Copenhagen and built a castle and observatory with the finest instruments for Tycho's use. The observatory was named Uraniborg, which means, "castle of the sky."

Tycho's observatory was the most bizarre observatory of all

time. It contained a ton of elaborate gold ornamentation. There were statues that both talked and turned on hidden mechanisms. The strangest observatory employee of all was an influential dwarf jester named Jepp. Tycho had an alchemy laboratory and furnace in the observatory. He was probably trying, like others before and after him, to turn cheaper metals into gold.

For 20 years Tycho, dressed in his finest robes, observed the heavens from Uraniborg. His observatory included the best-designed naked-eye instruments and followed the most accurate observing techniques of any observatory of its time.

His instruments were similar to those used by Ptolemy, but Tycho built his on a much larger scale. This made it easier to measure angles when looking through front and rear "gun" sights. His observatory instruments were many times more accurate in measuring angles than any other observatory instruments of his day.

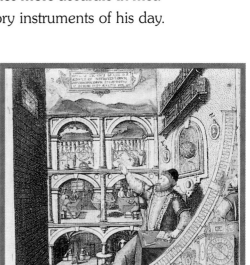

*This painting shows Tycho seated in his observatory and pointing to a small opening in the wall. Stars were seen through the opening. A moveable sight attached to the brass 90-degree arc mounted on the wall was used to measure a star's height above the horizon. A person seated at a table wrote down the measurements called out by Tycho. His dog sleeps at his feet.*

Tycho also believed that you could "Save the Phenomena" with high accuracy only when you knew with high accuracy the phenomena to be saved.

Tycho wasn't a Copernican. He offered his own model for the Universe, a compromise model that was part Copernicus and part Ptolemy. In Tycho's model, a central unmoving Earth was orbited by the Sun, which in turn was orbited by the planets. Tycho began to doubt Ptolemy's model when he observed the 1572 nova in Cassiopeia. Aristotle had said that changes in the heavens could not occur above the orbit of the Moon. But "Tycho's Star," as the nova became known, did occur there. Here was another instance where Aristotle and Ptolemy were shown to be wrong.

Unfortunately, Tycho died in 1601, eight years before Galileo first pointed his telescope toward the heavens. Fortunately, all of Tycho's valuable records were saved, including his years of observations of the movement of Mars. They were given to just the right person, Johannes Kepler.

## Mathematics—A New Eye on the Universe

Before he died, Tycho hired a young assistant named Johannes Kepler (1571–1630), an Austrian mathematician and high school teacher. Kepler had the worst eyesight of any observer of the heavens and was a very complex person. He was accident-prone and suffered from hypochondria (imaginary illnesses), myopia (nearsightedness), and polyopy (multiple vision). Kepler was also a mystic, a believer in mysteries and knowledge beyond ordinary human knowledge. For instance, he believed that the planets created sounds as they moved through the sky, a celestial harmony or "Music of the Spheres." He believed that because we hear this music at birth we are drawn to music later in life. He was a believer in astrology and was hired to cast and interpret horoscopes. He even used astrology to choose a wife. Kepler also wrote the first modern science-fiction book, *Somniun*, a dream of a journey to the Moon.

Kepler's eyesight was not a problem in his work. He was a new kind of astronomer with a new eye on the Universe. That eye was mathematics. He wasn't interested in looking into the heavens, he was interested in looking into the "mind of God" to learn about the Universe. He thought God was the supreme mathematician.

Kepler and Tycho were a wonderful pair of opposites. Tycho was an expert observer who collected mountains of information about the motion of the planet Mars in its orbit around the Sun. But Tycho had no idea how to use all that information. As an observer, Kepler could barely tell the difference between a star and a planet. But Kepler knew exactly what to do with Tycho's observations. Kepler used Tycho's Mars observations to discover the first accurate scientific laws describing how the planets and Earth moved around the Sun.

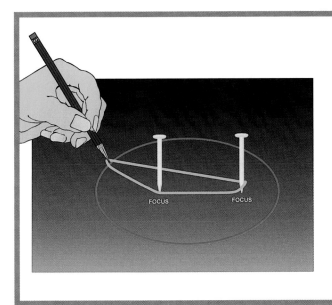

FOCUS          FOCUS

Kepler's first law says that the orbits of Earth and the planets are ellipses with the Sun at one focus point. Nothing is at the other focus point. An ellipse can be drawn around two nails with a loop of string. The nails mark the focus points of the ellipse. Find out what happens to the shape of the ellipse when the two focus points are moved farther apart or closer together.

Kepler began by upsetting Aristotle's idea that all heavenly bodies—including the planets—move in perfect circles. Kepler's first law stated that the orbits of the planets were *ellipses*, sort of egglike paths. His second law said that a line connecting the Sun and a planet swept out equal areas in equal times. Kepler's laws allowed him to very accurately predict future positions of planets. "Perfect" and steady circular motion and epicycles for the planets were gone from astronomy forever. Kepler, not Copernicus, created our modern view of the Solar System. We have said that old ideas die slowly. Galileo died still believing in circles and epicycles 33 years after Kepler's Laws appeared in his book called *The New Astronomy*.

Kepler's laws were a great accomplishment, but there was one big unanswered question about them: Why did they work?

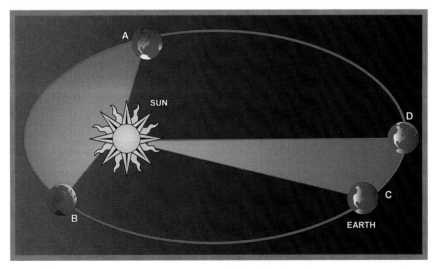

*Kepler's second law says that a line from Earth to the Sun sweeps out equal areas in equal time. The red area from **A** to **B** is equal to the red area from **C** to **D**. This means Earth moves faster from position **A** to **B** than from position **C** to **D**. When Earth is closer to the Sun it moves faster than when farther away.*

What force could cause the orbiting planets to follow Kepler's laws so perfectly? It took the greatest scientist of all time, Isaac Newton, to come up with an answer to that question.

## Newton Invents Gravity

Isaac Newton (1642–1727) was born on Christmas Day in 1642 on his family farm in Woolsthorpe, England. He was never known to be a very good student, either in the local schools or later at Cambridge University. But he was always known for his ability to concentrate his entire attention on something. Once while he was leading his horse back from the local market, the horse slipped out of its bridle. Newton was deep in thought and didn't know he had lost his horse until he returned home to find the horse waiting for him.

From 1665 to 1667 Cambridge University was closed. The students were sent home because an outbreak of the bubonic plague had spread from London to Cambridge. Thousands of people were dying every week in London. Newton returned to his family farm at Woolsthorpe. A famous story, that may not be true, tells of Newton sitting under an apple tree thinking about the Moon. He was asking himself, What keeps the Moon circling around Earth? An apple supposedly fell on his head and he had his answer. The same force that pulls apples to the ground pulls the Moon in an elliptical orbit around Earth. He called this force *gravity*. Young Newton then invented a new mathematics, called calculus, to understand more about the force of gravity as it reached out into space.

Newton's final answer to the problem explained why Kepler's laws worked. It is called the universal law of gravitation and has two parts. First, every object in the Universe attracts every other object. The force of attraction is greater for more massive objects, and weaker with less massive objects. The *mass* of an object is the amount of matter that it has. For instance, two whales in space would attract each other more strongly than two goldfish would. Second, the farther away from each other two objects are, the weaker the attraction between them. That is all you need to know to understand what holds the Universe together.

Newton had answered the most sought-after question of his

Isaac Newton, around 1700, and some objects of his genius. At right is the reflecting telescope he invented. At center is his book Principia, regarded as the greatest scientific book of all time. He holds a prism, with which he showed that white light actually is made up of all colors of the rainbow. His law of gravitation explained how the planets stay in orbit around the Sun, and how the Moon stays in orbit around Earth.

day, but then he forgot about it. He told no one. Newton was always very secretive about his discoveries.

Twenty years later the astronomer Edmond Halley (1656–1742) convinced Newton to let the world know about his theory of universal gravitation. Newton probably would have been happier working in his alchemy laboratory trying to make gold. But he agreed and published his ideas in 1687 in a book called *Mathematical Principles of Natural Philosophy*, or, for short, *Principia*. It became the most influential scientific book of all time. But a big question still remained. What was the cause of gravity? How could a force instantly act between two masses? And how could the masses involved measure each other's mass over great distances? Newton's theory didn't make a lot of sense, but it worked. When asked about it, Newton replied, "The cause of gravity is what I do not pretend to know."

The theory of gravity was mysterious, but since it worked, it was widely accepted. Newton's friend Halley was the first astronomer to use Newton's law of gravity to solve an astronomical problem. Halley worked out the orbits of what were thought to be three different comets and discovered that they actually were the same comet that kept coming back around the Sun every 76 years. He correctly predicted that the comet would return in 1758. When the comet came back right on schedule, it was named Halley's comet. Unfortunately, Halley died 16 years before that great day.

## A New Kind of Telescope

Gravity wasn't Newton's only contribution to astronomy. All astronomers, in all observatories, used refracting telescopes by Newton's time. But refracting telescopes, because they used lenses, suffered from annoying rainbow images. This problem is known as *chromatic aberration*, meaning color defect. Astronomers of the 1600s made their telescopes with the eyepiece as far from their light-collecting lens as possible. This produced the highest magnification and the least color-distorted image.

Johannes Hevelius (1611–1687), a Polish beer maker and astronomer carried this idea of a long telescope to an extreme. He made a 150-foot-long (46-meter) telescope that stretched over several housetops in his hometown of what is now Gdansk, Poland. The tube between the light-gathering lens at one end and the observer's eyepiece at the other end was made of wooden planks. The telescope was hung from a 90-foot-high (27-meter) mast to allow the telescope to be raised and lowered by ropes and pulleys managed by a team of assistants. "Aerial" telescopes of this type were cumbersome to use, and the slightest breeze would set the whole telescope swinging.

Try as he did, Newton failed to solve the lens color problem. However, he did manage to avoid the problem by inventing a new kind of telescope in 1688, called a Newtonian reflecting telescope. It used a curved, polished mirror to collect light at one end of the telescope tube. The observer's eyepiece was mounted on the side of the tube. It is the most popular type of telescope in use today.

The main interests of astronomers in the early 1700s were mapping the positions of stars for star catalogs, and the study of the planets, moons, and comets. Telescopes had increased the accuracy of the newer and larger star catalogs beyond that of Tycho's naked-eye abilities. For instance, Hevelius was mapping the positions of the stars and adding new constellations to the heavens. He also was mapping and naming features on the Moon.

Discoveries could be made with mathematics as well as with the telescope. With Kepler's laws of planetary motion and

Newton's theory of universal gravitation, mathematics had become another *eye* on the Universe. A parallax shift still had not been measured to *prove* that Earth circled the Sun, but all astronomers had come to accept the heliocentric model. Giant, reflecting telescope mirrors would next let astronomers see ever deeper into the unknown mysteries waiting in space. The attention of astronomers would move from the Solar System to the unexplored regions beyond. An age of discovery would begin with a musician-astronomer and his sister.

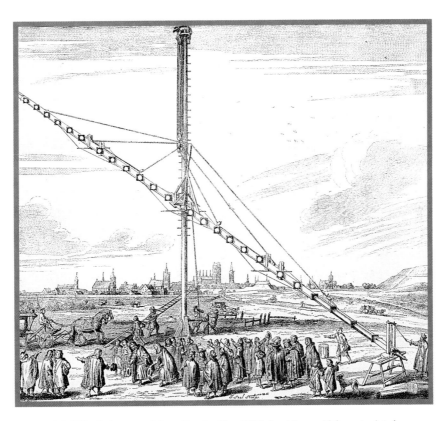

*Around 1650, Johannes Hevelius built a 150-foot-long (46-meter) telescope in an attempt to correct the color distortion creation by a single lens. It took several hours to put the telescope together before he could begin to observe. Hevelius was well known as an excellent observer of the stars.*

# Five

# An Age of Discovery

Mark Twain, author of *Tom Sawyer* and *Huckleberry Finn*, once said he never let school stand in the way of his education. The English astronomer William Herschel (1738–1822) never let his education stand in the way of his school either. His "school" was the star-filled, night sky. By training, he was an organist and music teacher. As an astronomer, Herschel was self-taught and an amateur. Because he was untrained, he looked into the night sky to see what was there, not to solve problems. Perhaps that's why he became such a great observer.

## The First New Planet

On March 13, 1781, Herschel, then 42 years old, peered into a 6-inch (15-centimeter) Newtonian reflecting telescope with a 7-foot-long (2-meter) tube. He had made the telescope himself and was continuing his second sky survey. He was studying the depths of space in a small area of the constellation Gemini the Twins. His eye and mind were suddenly drawn to a small patch of light "visibly larger" than the surrounding stars. He increased the telescope's magnification. Unlike a star, the image of the object was made to increase in size. When correctly identified, that small patch of light would bring him fame that would open the door to the world of professional astronomy. Herschel had discovered the first new planet in history.

He called his new planet Georgium Sidus, or "George's Star," in honor of England's King George III. Outside of England, it was not a popular name choice. This was because Herschel had discovered a planet and not a star, and because King George III had nothing to do with the discovery. The French astronomer Joseph Lalande suggested "Herschel" as a name for the new

*In 1781 William Herschel became the first person in history to discover a new planet, Uranus. "I perceived the visible planetary disk as soon as I looked at it," he wrote. His sister Caroline and son John also became famous astronomers. Herschel built his own telescopes, which were the best of the day.*

planet, but it was the German astronomer Johann Bode who picked the name that stuck—Uranus. In Greek mythology, Uranus was the god of the sky.

King George III requested that a Herschel-built telescope be demonstrated at his Royal Observatory in Greenwich. The king was very interested in astronomy and even had his own observatory south of London. Herschel waited nervously as the king's astronomers tested how sharply and how great a magnification his telescope would show different objects. One of the examiners was the king's Astronomer Royal, Nevil Maskelyne. Herschel was very excited when he heard that his telescope "exceeded in distinctness and magnifying power all they had seen before." As a result, Herschel was appointed a royal astronomer to the king and was given a small income. Herschel left behind his music career when he moved from the small summer resort city of Bath to the vicinity of the king's home at Windsor Castle. The king wanted Herschel and his telescope nearby so he could view the heavens whenever he wanted. William Herschel would remain a royal astronomer for the rest of his life.

## World's Largest Telescope

Night after night, year after year, Herschel studied the night sky through the large telescopes he built and set up behind Observatory House, where he lived near Windsor Castle. One telescope had a 48-inch (122-centimeter) mirror mounted in a 40-foot (12-meter) tube. For 56 years, from 1789 to 1845, it would be the largest telescope in the world. Observatory House became a tourist attraction and a sightseer's landmark. It also became the site of the greatest number of discoveries about the night sky in the history of astronomy. The greater size of Herschel's telescopic eyes allowed him to explore farther into space and make discoveries not possible by other astronomers. But Herschel did not ignore objects in space that were closer to home.

In 1718 Edmond Halley discovered that the so-called fixed stars were not fixed after all. He discovered that some of the brighter stars had very slowly changed position since the time of Hipparchus and Ptolemy nearly 2,000 years earlier. This real motion, or *proper motion*, of the stars can be seen only over long periods of time because of the stars' great distances. Why did the bright stars appear to move, but not the faint stars? Think of two airplanes, one much closer than the other, but each traveling at the same speed. The closer of the two airplanes will appear to be moving across the sky much faster. In the same way, if bright stars are closer than faint stars, then the bright stars will appear to move faster. Herschel was curious. If the stars of the night sky move through space, then does the Sun also move through space?

Herschel studied the proper motion of only 13 stars. He learned that in one part of the sky the stars seemed to be spreading out. In the opposite direction in the sky, the stars seemed to be coming together. This is what you observe of the landscape when you look out the front window and back window of an automobile as you move down a highway. Herschel concluded that the Sun was in motion carrying Earth and the entire Solar System with it in the direction of the constellation Hercules, where the stars appeared to be spreading out. In the opposite direction, in the constellation Orion, the stars seemed to be coming together as the Sun left them behind. These findings hold true to this day.

For more than 30 years Herschel studied the sky by night and built telescopes by day. His telescopes were of such excellent design, and so perfectly made, that the king's other astronomers were constantly amazed. Herschel's sister, Caroline, was his constant assistant at the telescope. She recorded every word as he

*Caroline Herschel was introduced to the stars by her father when she was a young girl. Later she became her brother William Herschel's assistant. She was the first woman to discover a comet, and she eventually discovered eight. A crater on the Moon was named after her.*

described the objects that swept into and out from his field of view. It was through the efforts of his devoted sister's copying, sorting, and editing his observations, plus the superior quality and size of his telescopes, that he was able to see what no other astronomer had seen before.

Caroline Herschel is often regarded as just an assistant to her brother, but she too was a very capable astronomer. She became the first woman to discover a comet. Eventually she discovered seven more comets and three nebulae. In 1835, when she was 85 years old, the Royal Astronomical Society presented her with its Gold Medal award in honor of her work. But she wrote in her memoirs "God knows what for."

In his lifetime Herschel made four detailed surveys of the northern skies. The extent and depth of his discoveries are hard to imagine as the work of only one person. Eventually, he discovered 269 double-star systems. *Double stars* are paired stars relatively close to each other. He also discovered that each star in a pair moved in orbit around the other, and that each followed Kepler's laws of motion. The two stars were held together as a pair by gravity. His discovery showed that Newton's law of gravitation worked far beyond the Solar System out to the most remotely known cosmic horizon.

## A Shape for the Milky Way

Herschel was also interested in the shape of the Universe. He and everyone else first thought the Universe was nothing more than all the stars of the Milky Way. Over several years, and using his 18-inch (45-centimeter) mirror reflecting telescope, Herschel counted the stars seen in small areas, off in different directions of the sky. He counted a lot of stars, but he did not count all of the 10 million stars he could see through his telescope. He called these star counts "star gauges." Herschel reasoned that areas crowded with stars extended farther out into space than areas containing fewer stars. He concluded that the Milky Way was a giant disk with the Sun near the middle. He later correctly suggested that some of the distant "clouds" he observed might be other Milky Ways of stars, or "island universes," far off in space.

Herschel made many other discoveries that broadened and sharpened our view of the Universe. He cataloged 2,500 nebulae, including a newly discovered type called a *planetary nebula*. The word nebula means "cloud." It describes best how these objects look in the telescope—like a planet. While some nebulae are clouds of gas and dust within our Milky Way Galaxy, others are galaxies very far away. A planetary nebula is actually a single star surrounded by a puffed-out gaseous atmosphere that the star has blown off into space. In a telescope it looks more like a planet than a star. Herschel also cataloged clusters of stars occupying

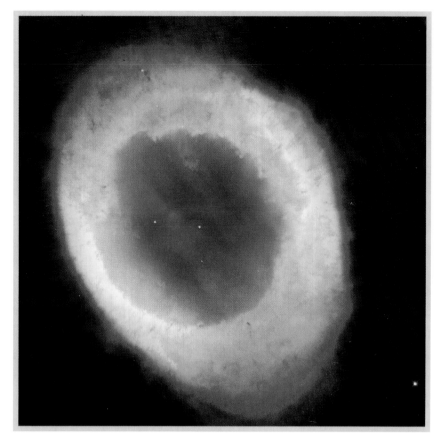

*Herschel was among the first to study so-called planetary nebulae, but these objects have nothing to do with planets. They are great clouds of gas and dust exploded off a star. This one is the Ring Nebula in the constellation Lyra the Harp. The star is at the Ring's center.*

small areas in space. Such a cluster may have as few as a dozen stars, or as many as 100,000 stars.

Could Herschel have accomplished more? Yes. In 1787 he discovered two moons of Uranus—Titania and Oberon. Two years later he discovered two moons of Saturn—Mimas and Enceladus. He also measured the periods of rotation of Jupiter and Saturn.

## Son Follows Father into Space

Herschel's son, John, extended his father's work into the night sky of the Southern Hemisphere. He set up the first observatory there at the base of Table Mountain in South Africa. For five years, he studied the largely unknown southern skies not visible from England using his father's 20-foot-long (6-meter) telescope with its 18-inch (45-centimeter) mirror. His work, like his father's, produced catalogs of new nebulae and star clusters as well as a catalog of double stars.

But it was another of John Herschel's interests that would give astronomy a new direction. He was interested in the then new craft called photography. To the younger Herschel we owe the words "photography," "photograph," "positive," and "negative" as applied to prints. His first photograph was of his father's 40-foot (12-meter) telescope. He also made the first photograph of the solar spectrum produced by a prism. Eventually cameras were attached to telescopes to photograph the night sky. Long exposures on photographic plates made accurate and lasting records that revealed stars and other objects too faint to be seen through even the largest telescopes not fitted with a camera.

No astronomer has discovered more new objects in the deep space of the night sky than William Herschel. A new planet, four new moons, double stars, nebulae, and star clusters were all his to explore because of the large size of his telescopic eye on the Universe. Hershel's list of contributions and discoveries was as big as his telescopes. But it was his discovery of "heat" energy from the Sun that would make future astronomers build new eyes to look even deeper into the Universe. The time had come to look *into* the Sun and other stars. It was time for astronomers to do what had been considered the impossible.

# Six

# Doing the Impossible

Isaac Newton closed the shades in his room and so opened a new window onto the Universe. While still a young student at Cambridge University, Newton placed a prism in a beam of light shining through a small hole in his drawn window shade. The result was a projected rainbow of colors. What he did next was most important. When the rainbow was passed through a second prism it re-created the original beam of white sunlight.

Newton had discovered the nature of sunlight. The white light *solar spectrum* consisted of the rainbow colors red, orange, yellow, green, blue, and violet. The different colors were caused by different wavelengths of radiation. Newton decided to add indigo as a seventh color, because seven was thought to have mystical properties and because the number appeared frequently in religious writings. No one, it turned out, agreed with his suggestion.

## The Spectroscope—Another New Eye on the Universe

In 1815 the German optical scientist Joseph von Fraunhofer invented an instrument called the *spectroscope*. Like a prism, the spectroscope separated sunlight into its different color wavelengths. But unlike a prism it also showed the solar spectrum crossed with many dark lines. What were they? This new instrument gave Fraunhofer a far more detailed, but puzzling, view of the light spectrum of the Sun than a simple glass prism. What caused the lines? To find out, Fraunhofer began to map the most prominent lines by assigning letters of the alphabet to them. Today we know them as *Fraunhofer lines*. Unfortunately, Fraunhofer never learned how to read meaning in this mysterious code in the light of the Sun.

Was it possible that Fraunhofer's lines could provide a clue to what the Sun was made of? Some scientists of the time scoffed at such an idea. In 1835 the famous French philosopher Auguste Comte stated that astronomers could look at the stars for as long as they wanted, but they would never know what they were made of. Why? Simply because they could never get a sample of a star to study in a chemistry laboratory. At the same time that Comte made his discouraging prediction, the German scientist Gustave Kirchoff was doing some experiments that, within a few years, would prove Comte wrong. You don't have to go to the stars for a sample, the stars are constantly sending samples of themselves to Earth.

Kirchoff made an important discovery. When heated and viewed through a spectroscope, each chemical element produced its own special pattern of bright lines along the color spectrum. These were not Fraunhofer's dark lines, but prominent bright lines. As he viewed one element after another, he found that its own "fingerprint" of bright lines could identify each element. Kirchoff then wondered if his bright lines might match Fraunhofer's dark lines. They did! At that point the Sun was brought into the laboratory for examination. The impossible had

**W**hen you see ocean waves you see the effect of energy moving through water. If the wave is high enough, the energy in the wave can pick you up and toss you around.

# Light: Energy in the Fast Lane

Sunlight, moonlight, and starlight can also be imagined as energy waves moving through space. But light waves move much faster than water waves. Nothing moves faster than light. Light energy travels at 186,000 miles (300,000 kilometers) per second. This is fast enough to circle Earth 7½ times every second. How fast is that? Hold your thumb out. Your thumb will be Earth. Now try to circle your thumb (Earth) with a finger on your other hand 7½ times in one second!

The distance between two successive wavecrests of light is called a *wavelength*. Our eyes see different wavelengths of light as different colors. We see the long wavelengths of light energy as the color red, and we see the short wavelengths as the color violet. The wavelengths of light energy shorter than red and longer than violet appear as orange, yellow, green, and blue light. All those wavelengths combined produce white light. As Newton had shown, a prism separates white light into its rainbow spread of colors, and another prism can recombine those colors as white light.

The total *radiation*, or energy, given off by objects in space, such as a star, includes more wavelengths than we can see with our eyes. The heat energy you feel from the Sun is *infrared radiation* of longer wavelengths than red. When you get sunburned, your skin is "burned" by *ultraviolet radiation*, which is energy of a shorter wavelength than violet.

*Light-energy waves traveling through space can be described just like energy waves traveling through water. The distance from peak to peak is called a wavelength. Our eyes see different wavelengths of visible light as different colors.*

been accomplished. The eye of the spectroscope made solar chemistry a part of astronomy.

In 1868 the English astronomer and science magazine publisher Norman Lockyer showed the added power of the spectroscope as a new eye on the Universe. During a total eclipse of the Sun, Lockyer observed lines in the Sun's spectrum that did not match the lines of any known element on Earth. Thinking he had discovered an element found only in the Sun, he named the element "helium," after the Greek god of the Sun, Helios. Twenty-seven years later the Scottish chemist William Ramsey discovered helium as a gas in Earth's atmosphere. Spectroscopy allowed a part of the air we breathe to be first discovered 93 million miles (150 million kilometers) away on the Sun.

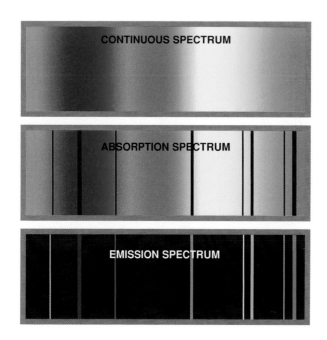

*There are three types of spectra. The continuous spectrum (top) shows all wavelengths. The absorption spectrum (middle) shows dark lines where wavelengths are absent because these wavelengths have been absorbed; for example, by the atmosphere.*

## Long-Distance Chemistry

Studying the distant stars through a spectroscope turned out to be more difficult than studying the Sun. The problem was getting enough light from a star to form a nice color spectrum. The Sun appears 145 million times brighter than the brightest-appearing star in the night sky, Sirius.

A pioneer in the early study of the chemistry of distant stars was another English amateur astronomer, William Huggins. In 1859 he decided to devote his life to astronomy. He sold his family cloth business and built his own private observatory. Huggins was especially interested in the use of photography with the spectroscope to study the stars. He felt that a photograph of a star's color spectrum would show more than just viewing the spectrum through a spectroscope attached to his telescope. At one stage, he realized that he needed an assistant for his observatory. So he married one. Margaret Huggins, it turned out, had similar research interests.

The Hugginses discovered spectral-line fingerprints for elements in the brighter stars that were the same elements found in the Sun. This was the first evidence for the "blind faith" belief that the Sun was a star and that stars were other suns. It also showed that the Universe was made of the same chemicals everywhere astronomers could then look. And wasn't it strange that many of those same chemicals made up the human body? What did it all mean?

Spectral lines revealed more than just what the stars were made of. Although Halley had shown that the stars moved through space, spectral lines showed *how* they moved through space, and how entire galaxies of stars moved through space. The key to learning about a star's motion came to be called the *Doppler effect*. And it was a key to what the Universe at large was doing.

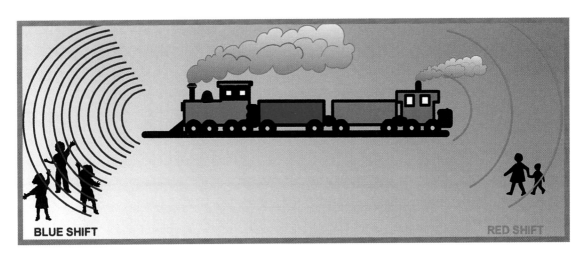

*The sound of a train coming toward you is different from the sound of a train moving away. When the train is coming toward you, the sound wavelengths are shorter than when the train is moving away. These shifts in wavelength are called blue and red Doppler shifts.*

Spectral lines show different wavelengths of a star's radiation. In the visible part of the spectrum—where the colors are—the wavelengths are longest at the red end and shortest at the blue-violet end. The *Doppler effect* is a shift in the position of spectral lines. This shift is due to a star's motion toward or away from Earth. The effect is named for the Austrian scientist Christian Doppler, who first explained it in 1842.

# The Doppler Effect:

## Why "Goodbye" Waves Are Longer Than "Hello" Waves

The spectral lines of a star, or galaxy, moving toward Earth bunch up and appear shorter than they would if Earth and the star were standing still. A shift toward the shorter (blue-violet) wavelength end of the spectrum is called a *blue shift*.

The spectral lines of a star moving away from Earth spread out and appear longer than they would if Earth and the star were standing still. A shift toward the longer wavelength end of the spectrum is called a *red shift*. Both a red shift and a blue shift are called a Doppler effect.

The Doppler effect is already familiar to you from the sound waves you hear. A blowing train horn that is speeding toward you will sound different after it has passed you and is speeding away. If you were in the train and moving along with the horn you would not hear any change. But when the train is approaching, the sound waves bunch up; when it passes, they spread out.

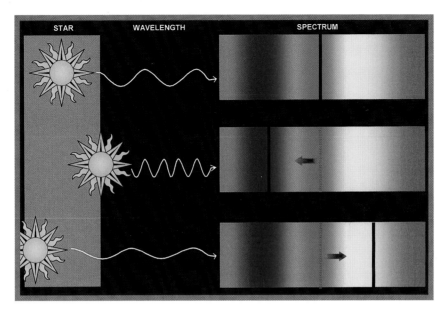

*The movement of a star toward or away from Earth changes the appearance of the star's spectrum. If a star is moving toward Earth (middle), lines in its spectrum show a shift toward the shorter blue wavelengths of the spectrum. If a star is moving away from Earth (bottom), lines in its spectrum show a shift toward the longer red wavelengths. If a star is not moving either toward or away from Earth, its spectral lines do not shift in either direction.*

## The Problem with the Galaxies

Our Milky Way home is a *galaxy* of more than 200 billion stars, but we can see only a tiny fraction of them. From space, the Milky Way would appear as a pinwheel disk 100,000 light-years in diameter and 3,000 light-years thick. The Sun would be a little more than halfway out from the central nucleus of the Milky Way and its outside edge. Astronomers use the light-year to measure great distances. A *light-year* is the distance that light travels in one year at the speed of 186,000 miles a second (300,000 kilometers). This distance is equal to 6 trillion miles (10 trillion kilometers).

There are enough stars in our galaxy for everyone in the

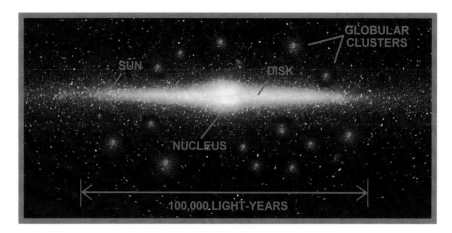

*The Milky Way galaxy, if seen from far out in space, would look like a thin disk of stars with a bulge at the center. It would be surrounded by a halo of individual globular clusters consisting of tens of thousands of stars each. The Sun is a star two-thirds the distance between the center nucleus and the outer edge of the disk.*

United States to own about 1,000 stars each. There are countless more galaxies, with countless more stars beyond the Milky Way. The story of their discovery began in 1750 with the questions of still another English amateur astronomer, Thomas Wright.

Wright began to ask if the small hazy patches of light seen in telescopes—nebulae—could be galaxies like our Milky Way, but at very great distances. Was our Milky Way just one part of a much larger universe? Astronomers took sides. Some thought the nebulae were island universes far beyond our Milky Way. Others thought they were just what they appeared to be—clouds of gas that were part of the Milky Way. The answer could be known only if the distance to a nebula could be measured. If the distance turned out to be greater than the size of the Milky Way, then the object had to be outside our galaxy.

The American astronomer Edwin Hubble (1889–1953)

finally answered the question. He had at one time been a boxer, a lawyer, and a soldier before he became the most famous astronomer of the 1900s. In 1924 he showed that some of the nebulae were, indeed, other faraway galaxies. They were part of a universe larger than most people had ever imagined.

Hubble used the 100-inch (2.5-meter) telescope at California's Mount Wilson Observatory. It was the world's largest telescope. He looked at individual stars in a nebula in the constellation Andromeda. Some of the stars he studied kept changing from dim to bright. These pulsing stars are called *variable stars*. Hubble watched a special type of variable stars, called *Cepheid variables*, go through their repeating periods of brightening and dimming. It was important that he know how the period of their change in brightness revealed their actual brightness. This allowed him to estimate the distance of the Andromeda Nebula. That distance measurement put the nebula way beyond the edge of the Milky Way. The Andromeda Nebula turned out to be a galaxy more than two million light-years away. That's more than 20 times the distance across the Milky Way.

*In 1924 Edwin Hubble showed that other galaxies existed far beyond the Milky Way. His work gave astronomers an important new view of the Universe. Although astronomers are not allowed to smoke in observatories, Hubble always like to be photographed with his pipe.*

*Around the year 1912 the American astronomer Henrietta Leavitt, of the Harvard College Observatory, discovered that the period of brightening and dimming of Cepheid variable stars was a key to their true brightness. That discovery enabled Hubble to estimate the distance to the Andromeda Galaxy.*

Since then, new galaxies keep being discovered. We now think that for every star in our Milky Way Galaxy, there may be a whole separate galaxy somewhere in the Universe.

What were all those galaxies doing? Were they just sitting there motionless, or were they moving around like the stars in our Milky Way? In 1922 the American astronomer Vesto Slipher was working at the Lowell Observatory in Arizona. It was an observatory built to answer the question about life on Mars. Slipher didn't answer that question, but he did answer the question about the motions of galaxies.

He said that almost all galaxies showed a red shift Doppler effect. That meant they were moving away from us! It was puzzling. Why should the galaxies be moving away from us? Did that also mean that the galaxies were also all moving away from each other?

Hubble next discovered that the greater the running-away speed of a galaxy, the greater its distance. That discovery became known as *Hubble's Law*. It seemed as if the Universe were expanding or getting larger. But what could be making the Universe expand? And if it were really expanding, would the galaxies keep running away from each other forever? It all seemed very puzzling.

The spectroscope had solved one "impossible" problem, detecting what the stars were made of, but then it created another problem—detecting that all the galaxies are rushing away from us. The color-spectrum fingerprints brought the Sun and stars into the laboratory. They showed that we, as humans, are all made of the same chemical elements as the Sun and distant stars. The spectroscope also showed that the Universe seemed to be expanding away from our galactic home. Did these two discoveries make us special? Did they put us in a *special* place in the Universe? Astronomers in ancient times would answer yes to both questions. But today's astronomers aren't quite so sure. They feel we would need more new eyes on the Universe to answer these questions. Those eyes are now in the making.

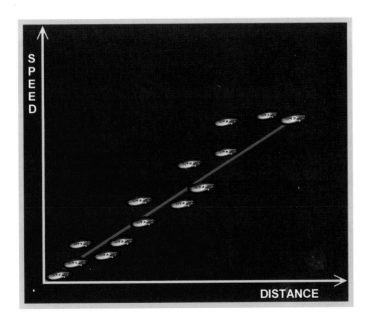

*Hubble discovered that the galaxies appeared to be rushing away from each other thusly causing the Universe to expand. He further discovered that the greater the distance of a galaxy, the faster it was speeding away. That rule became known as Hubble's Law. In the diagram, a galaxy halfway up the red line is speeding away and moving faster than a galaxy near the bottom of the red line.*

# Seven

# New Windows on the Universe

All discoveries in science are not the result of well-planned experiments. Sometimes accidents happen. William Herschel's discovery of infrared heat waves from the Sun was an accident, and so was the discovery of *radio waves* that shower Earth from space day and night. The discovery of the radio-wave window opened other windows as well. They were the windows needed to answer the question of what is happening in our Universe. The Universe was getting larger. But the event that could be making this happen was still unknown.

In 1931 Karl Jansky was a Bell Telephone Laboratories engineer trying to solve a problem. When people made phone calls between the United States and Europe, they often had trouble hearing each other because of static, or hissing noises. Jansky set up wire antennae mounted on a long, wooden platform that he could push around in a circle to try to find the cause of the static. He discovered that static was sometimes caused by thunderstorms, which didn't come as a surprise. But Jansky and everyone else were surprised at the second cause of the static: long-wavelength radio waves that were coming from the center of the Milky Way Galaxy.

## Astronomers Ignore Jansky's Discovery

Astronomers paid no attention to Jansky's discovery. Only a young ham radio operator and amateur astronomer, Grote Reber, was interested. In 1937 he built a 31-foot-diameter (9.5-meter) dish in his backyard that worked like the large mirror in a reflecting telescope. Its curved surface focused radio waves from space onto an antenna. It was the first radio telescope. His Wheaton, Illinois, neighbors thought it was a strange thing to have in his backyard and guessed it was some kind of a rainmaker. In his search for radio waves from beyond the Solar System, Reber managed to make a radio-wave map of the entire Milky Way Galaxy. Again, astronomers weren't interested.

It wasn't until after World War II that astronomers began to use the new radio technology developed during the war to look through the radio window at the Universe. Much larger radio telescopes were built. Astronomers soon found that the radio wavelengths of 21 centimeters discovered by Janksy were coming from cool hydrogen gas clouds within our galaxy. These gas clouds are invisible in optical telescopes since they do not give off visible light. The 21-centimeter wavelength discovery was also important because 90 percent of the Universe consists of hydrogen.

Astronomers soon came to realize that they had been missing important information about the Universe by looking only at the visible spectrum. If the long wavelength radio end of the *electromagnetic spectrum* held important invisible information about the Universe, then wouldn't the other end of the short wavelengths of ultraviolet, X rays, and gamma rays also hold

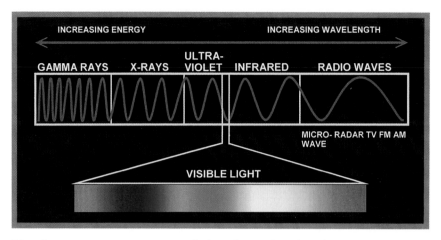

*The electromagnetic spectrum includes all wavelengths of radiation. Earth's atmosphere blocks out most of this radiation from space. However, some ultraviolet energy, visible light, and some radio wavelengths are able to reach Earth's surface.*

important information? The accidental discovery of radio waves from space was to open these other new windows and reveal the Universe in exciting new ways.

## Telescopes in Space

The new windows on the Universe were not easy to open. The ocean of air surrounding Earth blocks most radiation, except for light, radio wavelengths, and low-energy ultraviolet. To collect and study the wavelengths of X rays and gamma rays, for example, telescopes must be above the atmosphere, or at least above most of it. At first this was done by building observatories on mountaintops high above most of the air. Today infrared and visual astronomy are done at observatories such as the Mauna Kea Observatory on top of a high, inactive volcano in Hawaii. Balloons and high-flying airplanes were also used. But it has been satellite observatories put in orbit above virtually all of

Earth's air that have changed our understanding of our Universe the most. As in the past, these new eyes on the Universe have solved some mysteries, but have created others.

Satellite observatories and the equipment on board are expensive to build and put into orbit. Because of the cost, and because so many astronomers want to use them, astronomers now work in teams, whose members are often from different countries. Teams are the heroes now. The days of discoveries by individual astronomers such as Galileo, Herschel, Halley, and Hubble are gone.

In 1983 the first infrared orbiting observatory, the American-Dutch-British Infrared Astronomical Satellite (IRAS), was launched into a 560-mile-high (900-kilometer) orbit around Earth. The satellite carried a 22-inch (56-centimeter) telescope that had to be cooled to very low temperatures to collect infrared

*Pic du Midi Observatory is perched in the thin clear air above the clouds in the French Pyrenees Mountains. Other large observatories also are located high in the mountains. The Hubble Space Telescope has the advantage of being above all of Earth's atmosphere.*

wavelengths just longer than the visible red wavelengths. The mission of the IRAS "telescope in a thermos bottle" was to find low-temperature radiation sources. It found 200,000, including comets, *interstellar* dust clouds, and birthplaces of new stars in the Milky Way. IRAS even shared the discovery of a new comet.

The most exciting IRAS discovery was a disk around the bright star Vega, in the constellation Lyra the Harp. The disk showed the early creation of planets around Vega. Since then other telescopes have discovered planets around many other stars.

In 1978 the International Ultraviolet Explorer (IUE) was launched with an 18-inch-diameter (45-centimeter) telescope. In 1992 the Extreme Ultraviolet Explorer (EUVE) was launched

*Astronomers can examine galaxies, for instance, in different wavelengths of light. Here is the Andromeda Galaxy seen in ordinary light (left) and at infrared wavelengths (right). Infrared reveals hotter parts of the galaxy as red and cooler parts in blue.*

with four telescopes and special TV cameras. The mission of both satellites was to map the sky in wavelengths shorter than the visible violet wavelengths. These telescopes looked at the spectra of the hotter regions in space such as intensely hot white dwarf stars. *White dwarfs* are dying stars that have collapsed to the size of Earth.

The high-energy observatory satellites are designed to detect extremely short wavelengths to learn about the most explosive and most violent events going on in the Universe. X-ray and gamma-ray telescopes have been the most difficult to build. The usual mirror-type apparatus used to collect and reflect radiation cannot be used because X rays and gamma rays pass right through reflecting surfaces. In 1970 the first orbiting X ray observatory, Uhuru (Swahili for "Freedom"), was boosted into orbit. Its mission was to produce maps that showed what parts of space X rays were coming from. These puzzling sources are now thought to be exploding stars, exploding galaxies, and black holes. A *black hole* is a collapsed star so dense that its gravity prevents any radiation from escaping. We detect a black hole by the X rays emitted from a disk of gases that form around the black hole. The gases are pulled away from a companion star and are violently drawn into the black hole.

## A Two-Elephant School Bus in Space

In 1990 the Hubble Space Telescope (HST), built by the National Air and Space Agency (NASA) and the European Space Agency (ESA), was launched from the cargo bay of the space shuttle *Discovery*. It was placed in a 95-minute orbit 380 miles (600 kilometers) above Earth. The telescope was named after Edwin Hubble. The HST is the largest, most complex, and most powerful orbiting space observatory ever built. It is as big as a school bus and filled with telescope equipment the size of kitchen refrigerators. On Earth it weighed 12.5 tons, which is more than two African elephants.

The mission of Hubble is to take very detailed pictures and spectra of distant planets, clusters of stars, galaxies, and nebulae. The largest telescope on board is a 96-inch-diameter (2.4-meter) mirror that can collect visual, ultraviolet, and infrared wavelengths. HST also has cameras and spectroscopes. It can see objects 50 times fainter and with 10 times more detail than any telescope on Earth. As William Herschel's telescope did in its day, the HST has looked deeper into space and time than ever before. Hubble has more than expanded just our understanding of the Universe. Its photographs have expanded our amazement and appreciation of beauty in the Universe.

Understanding the Universe is like putting a puzzle together

*The Hubble Space Telescope was put into Earth orbit in 1990 to observe nearby space objects in the Solar System and objects out to the galaxies at the very edge of the Universe. Speeding at 17,500 miles an hour (28,000 kilometers an hour), HST circles Earth every 97 minutes at a height of 380 miles (600 kilometers). The gold colored panels collect energy from the Sun to power the telescope.*

The fingerlike columns of cool, dense gas and dust are regions where star birth is taking place in this eerie nebula, named the Eagle Nebula, 7,000 light-years from Earth. Stars are born when clouds of gas and dust collapse and form a sphere that heats up due to the force of gravity.

without knowing what the final picture will look like. Many different pieces from many different observatories on the ground and in space are needed to create the total picture. If we had to pick just one orbiting observatory as the one that has provided the most important piece of the puzzle, which one would it be? Probably the one called the Cosmic Orbiting Background Explorer (COBE), which was launched in 1989. It had one important job—to take the temperature of the Universe.

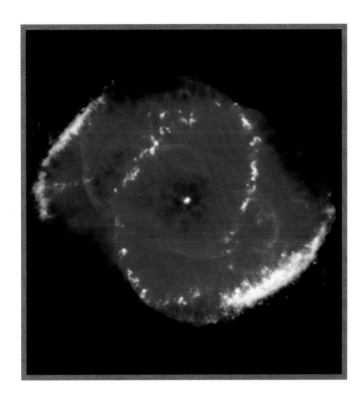

*The Cat's Eye planetary nebula, 3,000 light-years from Earth, is the result of an older star ejecting its outer gas layers to form a slowly expanding shell. The nebula looks like a ring, but actually is a spherical shell. Planetary nebula have nothing to do with planets. When they were first discovered, they were given that name because they looked round, like planets.*

## The "Day without a Yesterday"

By the late 1900s, most astronomers had pretty much accepted that the expansion of the Universe is taking place everywhere and causing all galaxies to appear to be moving away from all other galaxies. But the galaxies aren't actually moving away from each other; it is the increasing space between them that has the effect of pushing them apart. The galaxies are like dots on the surface of a balloon that is being blown up. The dots on the balloon move apart because the space between them is getting larger. We see red shifts of the galaxies due to this increase in the space between the galaxies.

If the Universe is becoming larger today, then at some time in the past something must have happened to cause the Universe to start expanding. It had to be a tremendous explosion. This explosion was the *Big Bang* and the beginning of space and time. It was called the "day without a yesterday" by the Belgian priest and mathematician Georges Lemaître. But can we be certain that such an explosion actually happened? Our reasoning goes something like this.

At the time of the Big Bang, the Universe had to be very hot. Then as it expanded it also had to cool, and keep on cooling to this day. Astronomers have tried to calculate just how cool the Universe should be today. If that predicted temperature turned out to be the same as the actual *background temperature of the Universe*, that would be pretty strong evidence that the Universe we know was due to a Big Bang creation in the distant past. So one key to the puzzle is knowing the background temperature, and that is what COBE was sent up to find out. When the answer came back, astronomers were excited.

The COBE-measured temperature of the Universe was the same as the temperature they had predicted! This was the strong evidence needed to support the idea that the expanding Universe of today started with a super hot Big Bang explosion perhaps 12 or so billion years ago.

Space satellite technology has changed astronomy and the way we view the Universe. It has allowed us to look through windows never before available. It has helped us to search back to the very creation of the Universe and the beginning of time.

Today we think we know at least something about the past history of the Universe, but what about its future? Will the Universe keep on expanding forever? Or will it eventually stop and come tumbling back in on itself and be born again? Will the Universe *ever* end? And a last very important question—are we the only ones in the Universe asking these questions?

# Eight

# Eyes on the Future

## An End in Fire or Ice?

We can imagine two ways the Universe might end—in fire or in ice. It would depend on how much mass there is in the Universe, including star matter, planets, comets, dust, everything.

If there is enough mass, then the force of gravity will first slow down and then stop the expansion. Like a ball thrown upward slowing down, stopping, and then falling to Earth's surface. The Universe would then collapse back into itself. As it did, it would heat up as giant collisions of galaxies and stars destroyed everything. The Universe would end in "fire," having begun with a Big Bang and ending with a Big Crunch. But just such an "ending" might turn into a new beginning since the Universe could return to the way it was at the time of its creation. Could a Big Bang happen again? Why not? And again? Why not? The Universe we know today could be just one cycle of a bouncing-ball cosmos that may have no beginning and no end.

But, suppose there is not enough mass to stop the expansion.

Then the Universe would go on expanding forever. The heat of the Universe would spread out through expanding space and make the Universe a colder and darker place, a deep-freeze cosmos.

So far as we can tell, the amount of mass in the visible Universe is only about 10 percent of the amount needed to stop the expansion. We seem to be heading into a cosmic ice age.

That might have been the answer for the end of the Universe except for a 10-year-old girl who in 1938 began to watch the constellations from her bedroom window in Washington, D.C. Over the years Vera Rubin kept up her interest in the night sky and became an astronomer, one who asked unusual questions. And her questions opened the door to one of the great mysteries of astronomy.

Rubin studied the motions of stars at the outer edges of galaxies. She discovered that the motions could be explained in only one way. There had to be a lot of invisible mass inside the galaxies, and that mass was exerting a gravitational tug on the stars at the outer edges. Astronomers now think there are two types of mass in the Universe. There is the mass that we can see, and there is mysterious *dark matter* that we can't see, not with any telescope at any wavelength. But we know it is out there because we can measure its gravitational tug. The visible mass is in the bright stars and galaxies, and anything else that is seen by telescopes and orbiting observatories.

How much of the mass of the Universe is unseen dark matter? Is there enough to stop the expansion of the Universe? The dark matter can be anywhere and everywhere. It can be out of sight in black holes and in the center of galaxies. It can be in thin clouds between the stars and galaxies. The only way to measure this dark matter is by its gravitational pull on the visible mass of the Universe. As time goes by, astronomers are discovering more and more dark matter. Some astronomers now think that 90 to 99 percent of the mass of the Universe is dark matter. If this is true, then everything we know about the Universe is limited to only about the 10 percent of it that we can see.

## Astronomers Are Problem People

The more we learn about the Universe, the less we seem to understand it. Each discovery creates new problems, but that's how science works. We find the galaxies grouped into *clusters*, and the clusters grouped into *superclusters*. The largest known collections of visible matter are clusters of superclusters. The American astronomers Margaret Geller and John Huchra discovered the clusters of superclusters only 65 years after Edwin Hubble showed that the Milky Way was not the only galaxy in the Universe! The clusters of superclusters are like the plastic in bubble wrap. They surround what appear to be large bubbles of empty space. Earth's nearest cluster of superclusters structure is called the *Great Wall*. It lies 330 million light-years away.

Even more mysterious is the *Great Attractor*. It is a mass with a gravitational pull equal to that of 10,000 or more galaxies the size of the Milky Way. Astronomers can't see the Great Attractor because it is blocked from view by dark clouds in our Milky Way Galaxy. But they know it exists because they can see clusters and superclusters being pulled toward it.

Are we the only ones pondering these problems? The most exciting discovery of all, in the future, may be learning that we are not the only sky watchers in the Universe.

Go out and gaze at the night sky Universe of the ancient sky watchers. It's yours for the looking, and it's the Universe of Hipparchus, of Copernicus, of Galileo, and the other astronomers who followed them. You don't even need a telescope. That part of the Universe you can see with your eyes is beautiful and mysterious. Gaze at it long enough and it will make you wonder about many things. Try to look into the night sky and not wonder if somewhere someone might be looking back.

*The giant dish of the 1,000-foot (300-meter) diameter radio telescope is made from 38,778 individual aluminum panels. It rests in a natural crater in the mountains of Puerto Rico. Too large to move, the radio telescope observes the sky as the sky passes overhead. The recording equipment hangs 50 stories high in the air above the dish.*

# Glossary

**Apparent brightness**—the brightness of a light source you can see in the night sky. Usually, the farther away the light source, the fainter it appears.

**Archaeoastronomy**—the study of the astronomical practices, structures, and beliefs of ancient cultures by looking at the placement and the way their buildings were constructed.

**Astrology**—the unscientific effort to link events in the sky, such as the positions of the Sun, Moon, and planets, with human events on Earth and the personal characteristics of individuals.

**Astronomy**—the science dealing with celestial bodies, their distances, brightness, sizes, motion, relative positions, composition, and structure. The word comes from the Greek language and means the "arrangement of stars."

**Background temperature of the Universe**—the temperature to which the Universe has cooled since the extremely hot Big Bang explosion that created the Universe some 12 billion years ago.

**Big Bang**—the model of the creation of the Universe, which says that the expansion of the Universe is taking place everywhere and causing all galaxies to move away from all other galaxies because of an explosion that was the beginning of space and time.

**Black hole**—an extremely dense star that has collapsed to such a small size that gravity prevents radiation from escaping its surroundings. X rays are emitted from the disk that forms around the black hole as matter is violently drawn into it.

**Blue shift**—the change of wavelengths toward the shorter (blue-violet) end of the spectrum because of decreasing distance between the source and observer.

**Cepheid variables**—stars that go through repeating periods of brightening and dimming.

**Chromatic aberration**—meaning "color defect." Lenses make rainbow images because of the different refracting or bending of the different colors of light.

**Cluster**—a group of a few dozen to hundreds or thousands of stars. Also refers to a group of a few dozen to hundreds or thousands of galaxies.

**Constellation**—a pattern made from bright stars in the night sky.

**Cosmic Orbiting Background Explorer (COBE)**—orbiting observatory that measured the temperature of the Universe and found it was the same as the predicted temperature. This was the strong evidence needed to support the idea of the Big Bang expanding Universe.

**Crescent**—the "C" shape of the Moon or a planet when less than half of it is seen lighted by the sun.

**Dark matter**—invisible matter in the Universe whose presence is known only by its gravitational pull.

**Deferent**—a circle moving with a steady motion around Earth at its center.

**Doppler effect**—an apparent change in the position of spectral lines. This change, or shift, is because of the motion of the stars and Earth. A red shift shows motion away and increasing distance between Earth and a star, or galaxy. A blue shift shows motion toward and decreasing distance between Earth and a star, or galaxy.

**Double star**—two stars held together by gravity with each revolving around a common center point. Also called binary stars.

**Electromagnetic spectrum**—different wavelengths of electric and magnetic energy traveling through space. The full range of wavelengths includes radio waves, infrared, visible light, ultraviolet, gamma, and X rays.

**Ellipse**—an elongated "circlelike" or oval shape. This is the shape of the path of the planets as they revolve around the Sun.

**Epicycle**—a circle moving with a steady motion with its center on a deferent. The Sun, Moon, and planets were placed on epicycles.

**Extraterrestrial**—meaning from outside or "beyond Earth."

**Extreme Ultraviolet Explorer (EUVE)**—orbiting observatory to map wavelengths shorter than the visible violet wavelengths.

**Fixed stars**—stars that do not move in relation to one another. The constellations are made up of fixed stars.

**Fraunhofer lines**—dark lines seen crossing a spectrum when using a prismlike instrument called a spectroscope. The lines tell about the chemical composition and movement of the source of the spectrum.

**Galaxy**—a vast collection of stars, gas, and dust held together by gravity.

**Geocentric**—meaning "Earth-centered." This was the idea of the Universe that Aristotle and Ptolemy believed in.

**Gibbous**—the shape of the Moon or a planet when more than half of it is seen lighted by the Sun.

**Gnomon**—the shadow-casting pointer of a sundial that follows the motion of the Sun across the sky.

**Gravity**—a pull or force between bodies that depends upon the masses of the bodies and their distances. The more massive the bodies the greater the force. The farther the bodies move apart, the less the force.

**Great Attractor**—an especially massive collection of galaxies that we cannot see but which we can detect as a result of its gravitational attraction. The strength of its gravitational pull suggests that it may contain 10,000 galaxies the size of the Milky Way.

**Great Wall**—a cluster of superclusters of galaxies some 30 times broader than it is thick. Its shape suggested its name.Hairy star—a name given to a comet because the comet's tail looks like flowing hair.

**Heliocentric**—meaning "Sun-centered." This was the idea of the Universe that Aristarchus and Copernicus believed in, and the way the Solar System is described today.

**Hubble's Law**—the farther a galaxy is from the Milky Way the larger its red shift Doppler effect. This is due to the increasing distances between galaxies because of the expansion of the Universe.

**Hubble Space Telescope (HST)**—the largest, most complex, and most powerful orbiting space observatory. The mission of Hubble is to take very detailed pictures and spectra of distant planets, clusters of stars, galaxies, and nebulae.

**Infrared Astronomical Satellite (IRAS)**—orbiting observatory sent into Earth orbit to collect infrared wavelengths just longer than the red wavelengths visible to our eyes.

**Infrared radiation**—invisible wavelengths that are a little larger than the red wavelengths at one end of the visible spectrum. Infrared wavelengths are felt as heat.

**International Ultraviolet Explorer (IUE)**—observatory sent into Earth orbit to collect ultraviolet wavelengths just shorter than the violet wavelengths visible to our eyes.

**Interstellar**—meaning "between the stars."

**Light-year**—the distance light travels in one year, at the rate of 186,00 miles (300,000 kilometers) per second, which is about 6 trillion miles (10 trillion kilometers).

**Mass**—the quantity of material a body has. It is related to weight on Earth, but it is not the same as weight. In space a body can be weightless, but it will still have mass. It will have the same amount of material as on Earth.

**Milky Way**—the name of our local galaxy, containing some 300 billion to 500 billion or more stars. Also the name of the hazy band of light seen in the summer and winter sky. A small telescope shows the band as a region of countless stars.

**Model**—an idea of the way something works.

**Nebula**—meaning "cloud." A great cloud of dust and gas within a galaxy.

**Newtonian reflecting telescope**—uses a curved mirror to collect light. The eyepiece is on the side of the telescope tube.

**Nova**—a "new" star that appears in the night sky from light produced by an exploding star. The star was too far away and too faint to been seen before the explosion.

**Omen**—something that is used to predict a good or bad future event.

**Parallax shift**—a change in the position of distant stars because of the movement of Earth around the Sun. The farther the star, the smaller the parallax shift.

**Planet**—a celestial object that shines by reflected light from a star around which the planet is held by gravitational force.

**Planetary nebula**—a nebula that looks round like a planet when seen through a telescope.

**Precession**—a wobbly motion of Earth caused by the gravitational pull of the Sun and Moon. It changes the position of the north pole in the sky.

**Proper motion**—the actual change in a star's position as it moves through space.

**Radiation**—the energy given off by objects.

**Radio waves**—long-wavelength radiation able to pass through Earth's air.

**Red shift**—the change of wavelengths toward the longer (red) end of the spectrum because of increasing distance between the source and observer.

**Retrograde**—the "backward" motion of a planet that is different from the planet's normal west-to-east motion through the fixed stars.

**Revolve**—the motion of one object around another object. Earth and the planets revolve around the Sun.

**Rotate**—the spinning of an object. Earth rotates 360 degrees every 24 hours.

**"Save the Phenomena"**—Plato's assignment to his students, asking them to devise a model of the Universe that would explain everything they saw in the night sky.

**Shooting star**—the flash of light made by a sand-sized particle from space as it burns up due to friction with Earth's atmosphere. Shooting stars are sometimes called "falling stars." Shooting stars and falling stars are not really stars.

**Solar spectrum**—the individual wavelengths of energy received from the Sun. The visible part includes the colors red, orange, yellow, green, blue, and violet.

**Spectroscope**—a prismlike instrument that shows the solar spectrum crossed with many dark lines.

**Spectrum**—the range of individual wavelengths from a source of radiation such as the white light from the Sun.

**Star**—a large hot, glowing globe of gases that emits energy through a process called nuclear fusion. The Sun is a typical, and our closest, star.

**Supercluster**—a cluster of clusters of galaxies.

**Ultraviolet radiation**—invisible wavelengths that are a little smaller than the blue-violet color (short wavelength) at the end of the visible spectrum. Ultraviolet wavelengths cause sunburn.

**Variable stars**—stars that go through periods of brightening and dimming that are related to the actual brightness of the star.

**Wandering stars**—the planets appear as starlike objects that wander or move through the background of fixed stars. The fixed stars are the zodiac constellations.

**Wavelength**—the distance between two successive wave crests.

**White dwarf**—a star that has collapsed to the size of Earth and is slowly cooling.

# Further Reading

Achenbach, Joel. "Life Beyond Earth." *National Geographic*. January 2000. pp. 24–51.

Burnham, Robert, and Gabrielle Walker. *Astronomy*. Pleasantville, NY: Reader's Digest, 1998.

Dickinson, Terence. *Nightwatch: A Practical Guide to Viewing the Universe*. Buffalo, NY: Firefly, 1998.

Ethier, Bryan. *Fly Me to the Moon: Lost in Space with the Mercury Generation*.Tampa, FL: McGregor, 1999.

Gallant, Roy A. *Earth's Place in Space*. Tarrytown, NY: Marshall Cavendish, 2000.

Hathaway, Nancy. *The Friendly Guide to the Universe: A Down-to-Earth Tour of Space, Time and the Wonders of the Universe*. New York: Penguin, 1995.

Hennessey, R.A.S. "Thomas Dick's Sublime Science." *Sky & Telescope*. February 2000, pp. 46–49.

Mammana, Dennis. *Star Hunters: The Quest to Discover the Secrets of the Universe*. New York: Running Press/Friedman Group, 1990.

Morrison, Phillip, and Phylis Morrison. *Powers of Ten*. New York: Freeman & Co, 1994.

Naeye, Robert. "Looking for Life." *Astronomy*, December 1999, pp. 45–47.

Panek, Richard. *Seeing and Believing: How the Telescope Opened Our Eyes and Minds to the Heavens*. New York: Penguin, 1998.

Raymo, Chet. *365 Starry Nights*. New York: Prentice Hall Press, 1986.

Reed, George. *Dark Sky Legacy*. Buffalo, NY: Prometheus Press, 1989.

Schilling, Govert. "Giant Eyes on the Sky." *Astronomy*. December 1999, pp. 49–51.

Page numbers for illustrations are in **boldface**.